I Define Madness

This is dedicated to all of those who gave me valuable lessons on life, love, and happiness. For those who supported me and motivated me to be the vibrant being that I am. These words reflect who I was and who I am growing to be. An accomplishment of my ages, much love and happiness be to all of you!

It is a rigid and loving complimentary compendium of experiences by me and of my life as well as spreading the message that even in your darkest of hours, everything will be okay!

IDM

Contents

Misery, It loves company…… 7- 20

The Mold to Madness ……... 23-48

Bittersweet …………………. 51-82

Acceptance …………………. 85-148

Be Still My Soul ……………. 151-164

Break the Chains…………… 167-187

Creator……………………… 191-225

Destiny ……………………… 230-271

Misery, it loves company

Reconciliation

I waited for you;

But, no one knew.

Waited just to know,

And now, it's time to let it go.

Years mean nothing in retrospect,

When moments were needed just to reconnect.

Didn't want to give such effort,

So many years, so many records.

Wasted time, all those moments;

On your own time, sparing no innocence.

We wasted all ours of the night,

For once, I just needed to confide.

No one there, listening nor waiting,

Don't even know what's worth contemplating.

A battle, so tired; never ceasing

A war; ever increasing.

Letting go of all our ties,

All the pain, will soon subside,

A broken life, yours until you die.

Uplifted, such a blissful feeling,

Unknown that this would be so freeing.

No stress, just smiles,

Goodbye my "friend",

I wish to not reconcile.

May peace and love follow you,

In the end, there was nothing to lose.

US

Detachment sets in,

Well hello;

My

Dear

Friend.

Our secret,

Is our passion now.

I love it how you hold me down;

Bite

My lips harder.

Things have changed;

My view

Of you

So strange.

It's paradoxical; a ticking time bomb.

It feels

So

Right

Knowing that it's so wrong.

Common interests;

Not so different,

Are we?

Break the mold,

We will discover the

Us

That no one else knows.

MELANCHOLY

Even on the cloudy days;

I can't shake

Those thoughts,

Of you

SWEET ADDICTION

Like a moth to the flames,

I'm addicted to the pain.

See the pleasure in your eyes,

My departure is no surprise.

Watch you fade to the black,

Keeping distant, watch your back.

Listening for the silence,

Yearning for such violence.

When you tie me up?

Slam me down,

If only you knew, the demon that you had found.

I want to feel you, trusting, you'll be back again.

Watching, waiting, until you take control;

Again.

3:15 AM

Demons throwing stones in my head,

Making angels in the sheets upon my bed.

Twisted spirals, tainted hues;

Melancholy life of the used,

Radiantly effervescent, shining so bright

Inadvertently, so bad yet so damned right.

Such sweet nothings;

Tantalizing all my dreams,

Falling short of blissful misery.

Tainted by the thought of thee,

Broken down but not distraught.

Lesson from the pain, where memory is naught.

GONE AGAIN

Out of nowhere,

You're there;

But then,

In another moment,

You're gone again.

LOVE UNENDING

The lake shaped like a crescent moon,
Filled with the tears of fallen and departed.
Once in a fortnight it shades with blood,
A bath for the fallen,
Once loved, now long forgotten;
In days of old, the people prayed,
For them to find a holy place;
That they are forgiven of mistakes once made.
Passing to a new life after the grave.
But what of love never ending?
When darkness pours within the waters,
Taking true form,
Old wise men and dearly departed,
Rise once again, to mourn.
She comes again each night,
"come with me my love,
Bathe within this pool of blood,
Rise with the moon and dance in the sun,
Angel of light, my darling, my love".
Drown in the waters of sin,
Heart beats, awaiting his return again.

TEN STORIES

Can you hear me screaming from the top of a ten-story deathbed?

Can you see me falling, from all the words that you've said?

Can't you feel my heartbeat racing faster, faster, and faster?

As I'm laying my head on your chest, fingers wrapped around me,

And I know, and I know, this is where I want to be, forever; or is this merely just a dream?

Is this another reality?

When I open my eyes from such a slumber, will you be with me?

Or will this be my last breath, lingering in the stillness of your serenity?

This is never ending, never ending dream;

The only place to see your face,

The one way that I can feel your embrace.

LAST TIME

Put on that mask that you wear,

Go about living in fear.

Nothing changes, it never will.

Just for one chance at love, you would kill;

Your heart, it's breaking.

Like a mirror, the shards fall to the floor;

Blood running from those beautiful wrists,

This is the last time, the last time.

So you put on that mask that you wear,

Cover that pretty face with your hair.

Go out into the world,

What are you scared of, beautiful girl?

Tears always dwelling in those eyes,

In your mind, are thoughts of suicide.

Tired of waiting, searching for someone.

Tired of crying, crying for anyone;

Screaming your heart out, but no one hears you,

Crying those eyes out, no one sees you.

To them it's just a game; a game we all play.

In the end we're all the same, all having someone to blame.

Pretty girl, thinking of his smile;

Pretty girl, living in denial.

Gave it all up, in the end it's still the same.

Why are you so afraid, yet still kiss skin with that blade?

All that's left are memories on the wall;

As you're in the ground, there's one who recalls.

All the love that you wished for, he yearned for yours more;

Life's not the same now, pretty girl; you were his world.

BITTERSWEET

The desolate night hearkens,

Fruitful and effervescent, lavish with emotions.

As daytime loneliness fades away,

Here and now, fears have all but remained.

A cry of clairvoyant ecstasy,

Amidst the vivid and flourishing emotion.

A raw sense of unbeknownst passion arises,

Like the calm before the store, bittersweet.

Take it to another level, thriving between;

Tangled up within another, two become one.

Just once more, a masterpiece of devotion.

LET ME

Maybe I'm over-zealous,

Or maybe, I'm just jealous.

It could sound quite pretentious,

But I can't stop thinking about us.

The way you're wrapped around me,

You're everything I thought I'd need.

Such bliss cannot just be found.

Two souls intertwined,

Ascended form the hands of time.

Never met someone so divine.

Please say you love me too,

Just let me love you.

FALL

Loved and lost,

What a tool.

Maybe just lost,

What about you?

Did you even love yourself?

You lost too, love.

Just you, no one else matters;

When you fall.

QUICKSAND

Misery loves company,

One day you'll understand.

Their words are quicksand,

To kill all your joy.

In order to relate;

They'd keep you in this state.

They do it unknowing,

Ever so deceiving,

They'd much rather watch you bleeding.

THE MOTIONS

I'm better,

I'm sorry,

I am happy,

I am crying,

I am moving on,

I am dreaming of you.

I am past this,

I am on my knees,

I can't do this,

The only thing that separates;

Is the pride and the ego.

THE VOID

The day will come,

Face to face,

Real emotion,

No holding back,

I love you, still.

But even empty words,

Won't fill the void.

3:01 AM

You were more than enough;

But then you stopped trying.

And settled for denial,

Now all you do is cry,

You're still someone's everything.

DON'T

When the night comes,

Will you think of me?

When everything is said and done,

Will you be by my side?

They'll do what they can,

To tear us apart,

Will you listen?

Will you leave me alone?

We choose our own paths.

Our own faith to live with,

Don't give in,

Don't leave,

I would have given everything for you.

Walk through hell to hold you,

Seeing you smile,

Was all that kept me going.

(and now that's gone)

HEAVEN

Daydreaming again,

In a field so full of flowers,

Blossoming in the sun,

Dancing as rain kisses their petals.

She smiles again,

His heart, it feels heavy now;

Did she go to heaven?

Eyes clouded with tears,

Will they ever meet again?

Hold gazes upon one another,

There in the other's arms,

Forever as the days pass.

She lays there,

Free from all that once bound her.

Holding her hand, the last time,

He lets her go.

It's been a year now,

And he's still daydreaming.

In that field of flowers,

Did she go to heaven?

THE DIFFERENCE

I'd pour out my soul;

It wouldn't make a difference,

Fall to my knees, asking forgiveness.

Nothing would matter anymore,

One mistake too many,

I may never learn.

Go around, acting as if it's none of my concern.

I never meant to hurt you,

The one who was always there,

I threw it in your face,

No steps left to retrace.

Just hear me, I am sorry for everything.

I may never get better,

I can't tell you goodbye,

Need you in my life.

Don't blame you, just walk away.

THE PRESSURE

The way my heart beats faster,

The way my body acts,

When you're around,

None of it really matters.

You're in love with her,

And I'm on the sidelines,

Wishing you loved me…

The Mold to Madness

THING

What is a name,

A name for a thing?

Are you a thing?

With a heartbeat so stale,

Are you a name or a thing?

Or merely a name for a thing?

MIND

It's a dark place,

That mind of yours,

It's a scary place,

To try and endure.

But you've made it a home,

You've made it on your own.

THE IMPALER

There is a forest I see in dreams,

Darkened by the forms shaped as trees.

The feeling isn't the same,

An odd aroma fills the air,

Stagnant as the bodies slowly decay.

Blood pours as if rain from the sky,

Another scream, another cries.

Laughter echoes freely within this forest,

Feeling that steely gaze upon me,

A face that burns deep within my mind.

Bending them to his undying and forsaken will,

Upon refusal, they are slowly broken.

Impaled for their indignity, humanistic dishonesty,

By the wrath of a "god"

So I stay here wondering, within the forest of damned souls,

Irregular as may be, the blood drips from these trees;

As he sits there, cup in hand gazing upon his masterpiece.

There I stand, in the forest of the freed.

HOLLOW

These games that you play,

Thoughtless, hollow words that you'd say.

Lacking any emotion, irrationally oblivious;

Suffering consternation of such a commitment.

Forsaken by your own manifestation of desire,

Yearning for everything, plotting and conspiring.

You can't have it all, loving and so vivacious;

You can't have her, an unapproachable ideal.

Quintessentially the most remarkable individual.

Apprehensive, withdrawing to acknowledge the principle.

You receive only what you give, strain to attain your desires;

Or wither away slowly, receding into the nihility.

A NIGHT LIKE THIS

I hate liars, but love hypocrites.

Something to keep me going on a night like this!

All hail the blasphemy that drowns the crowds,

Let me demonstrate, as the truth surely confounds.

And the weak fall to their knees,

Yearning freedom, yet cry out for someone to lead;

Discerning, yet they see one thing.

Wear your mask and go on parading as their king,

I'll be here when you succumb to the pressure.

Watching and waiting in sheer pleasure,

And the skies will light with a new dawn, such sweet bliss;

Oh how I hate liars but fall in love with such hypocrites!

STORIES

I make up stories,

Just to pass the time.

Please do not worry,

Not all of them are made to rhyme.

I have no worries left for this life,

No battles left to be fought.

I'll carry on with no such sorrow,

Memories were never made to be forgotten,

Always a purpose for the lessons.

Some hidden, some in the open;

A moral for each one told,

A dreamer is meant to be awoken,

Rivers rage, oceans calm;

Telling us of times that are long past.

May never know the true meaning,

Be happy with what you have while it lasts.

Friendships made; others severed.

Spaces between, fights started;

Always thinking that we're the only ones,

Going through tragedy and heartbreak.

Such a shame;

Put ourselves through all this pain.

GLORY

Making it harder than it is,

A glimpse of what's past.

Memories built upon a destructive ego;

Beauty that once eternally raptured.

Sweet decadence brought upon yourself.

Age standing as the only cripple,

An internal battle wages; in the estranged mind of genius,

A never-ending war, blind to the untrained.

Playing tricks on your mind;

Are you alive?

Unannounced and unknowing, it slithers within.

Devouring your humanity; you won't last long.

Only time will truly tell; the ending of the story,

Alas you must choose; your life or this new-found glory?

3 AM

I tried so many times,

Tried but couldn't.

Another notch upon my list,

Another unobtainable wisp.

Maybe I grow dumb, weak, feeble;

In age, the end is unforeseeable.

Try, try as you might;

These fickle hands run tight.

Tick tock, tick tock;

Turning are the hands, that clock.

From birth, celebrate the mourning;

Only time will tell, the fate that's forming.

Free the fickle hands of fate,

who are we to make them wait?

Open arms adorn so warming,

My love for them, ever conforming.

WANTING

You've been found wanting more.

Nothing is ever enough to pacify,

Such a sad life,

Nothing is ever worthwhile.

FACE

PULL MY FINGER!

Don't do it, too late;

A perfect moment of flatulence.

I warned you, didn't I?

HIGH FIVE!

In your face,

You missed,

What a dick.

UNDONE

Your smile,

You wear it well.

A perfect mask,

For your denial.

Great job,

Well done,

When the curtain falls,

You'll come undone.

ALWAYS

He will come back,

They always do.

But when he does,

What will you choose?

DELIRIOUS

Are you a monkey or a man?

A monkey man.

So basic, say complicated? Over rated!

Primal instincts that drive you.

Animalistic, so true!

Parade around acting civil,

You're just a basic animal.

Beat your chest, act tough!

So fake, so glad I called your bluff!

FAT CAT

Pat, pat, pat;

The steps of a cat.

Heavily she treads,

Turning heads,

Panting with the motion.

Jarring things, such commotion!

The struggle is real,

Could be related to Garfield.

How extraordinary is that?

But she is just a fat cat.

COCO

I love the way,

you melt in my mouth.

The mere thought,

It drives me crazy,

Throat tightens, lips quivering.

Just want you in my hands,

All over,

In the cold winter day,

There's nothing like chocolate.

PRIDE

Be patient,

Just wait.

He will realize his mistake;

Come crawling back,

When pride has died.

EGO

You're not happy,

Are you?

Wear that mask like a crown,

Those thorns are deadly, you know.

A GREAT IDEA

I'm happy that you're mine,

I lied.

I'll always have your back,

until you break, I lied.

I'm not like the others,

Should have listened to mother,

I love you,

Only what you do.

A great idea,

You,

I was drunk.

But I like you,

Wait for me,

Never mind.

You were right,

You're a catch, I should hold on;

I was drunk.

Friends for life,

You were right,

I lied.

MYSTERY

Can a butterfly,

Lie?

As it flies to the sky,

From grounding;

Ascension to true purpose,

Or deceit?

SHATTERED

Try as I will,

May I never succeed.

Efforts gunned down,

Before you'd believe.

Try as I might,

Never will it matter.

Broken and shattered;

Strength is now gone,

Shadows now, where the light would weave.

Darkness is all, it would seem;

Falling into ways of old,

Depression takes its toll,

A smile on my face.

But they don't know,

The real me.

WAITING

Images fade,

Time flies by.

Each blade of grass,

Will always die;

We'll all be waiting,

Until you return.

Come back to us,

Speak what you've learned,

How broken is our world?

Life still moves on,

Unite us now.

Bring us your strength,

Merciful tyrant.

Leading us down,

Into our demise.

DELIVERANCE

A darkness,

It clouds the sun.

Hearts grow slowly,

Colder than ice.

Nothing can slow the coming;

No-where left to hide.

From the hatred,

That's buried deep inside.

No even a heart so pure,

Or an angel's soul,

Can stop the deliverance;

Of self-made,

Actions.

DISPOSITION

Things have changed,

But, I'm still the same.

Living in the shadows,

Of those who think they matter.

Take a sip of my poison,

My magic potion,

Casting away all doubts.

You're under my spell now,

Believing things as they were.

Forgetting all your wrong turns,

You belong to me now,

Angel of dark temptations.

VANITY

Colors of red, purple, and blue.

Taunting and pulling you down,

Gazing upon the image,

You in that wedding gown.

Nothing can change it;

Can't hide it,

You yearn to be like them.

You'll always be useless,

Crying in those closets,

No one can hear you scream.

"Why can't I be like them?

Oh Vanity!"

Yearning to shed those pounds.

Starving yourself now,

You're beautiful the way you are.

Please don't give up your sanity,

For the sake of vanity.

MASS

The midnight mass is waiting,

For your arrival.

Trees dressed in blood; it's dripping.

Earth sheathed with corpses,

This is your last time, last try.

Baby, you'll never survive;

Should never have come here.

Already told you; leave.

Didn't heed the warnings,

Your last night alive,

Mass is in session!

THIS WORLD

Stuck in a time and place,

Where one looks away from on in need.

Shallow, empty hearts and souls,

Consumed with hate and greed.

How has it come to this?

Wondering from place to place,

New challenges come to mind.

Will this world ever change?

Broken hearts left in unrest,

Tainted spirits surround me.

Watching as the other struggles,

Can't they hear those helpless screams?

Bittersweet

2:59 AM

Can still feel your kiss,

On my lips.

Is it too much?

To ask for,

A forever just like this.

SUCCULENT

With your hands around my neck,

I am complete.

My trust I give you,

For a night of bliss.

LOVE AND DEATH

One day?

Fuck that.

Why not today?

Yesterday?

One day.

You'll smile;

Love,

Die,

Don't wait for another day.

Just someday,

Enjoy today,

Before you waste away.

NOT

You smile again,

I walk away.

You speak again,

Not today.

I'm not your SOMEDAY.

Not yesterday, today, or any other day.

I am me,

If you had seen,

But now it's too late.

THE GAME

It's just how it happens,

I move on.

You come right back,

You move on.

And I'm waiting,

How do we get past it?

Piece by piece, brick by brick.

TOO COOL

Picture perfect,

That's us!

On the back of the bus,

Too cool for school.

Obvious with "perfect" attendance,

"it's just a phase".

I'd love to relive those days!

FRIENDS

I don't do this very often,

True friends are hard to find.

That no matter what,

You'll be there when I cry.

JOURNAL

Life and love,

Isn't always about souls.

About falling into a bed of roses,

Sometimes, it's the pieces;

Of you and them,

That makes the two a whole,

And no one knows.

Where you're going in this journey,

Finding one, you find three.

So just one of them could see,

Then they leave, but you keep connecting.

To make peace eternal,

You keep the pace, in a journal.

UNKNOWN

Love-sick, missing my compass;

Never knew it would come to this.

Forever in the unknown,

The warning signs never shown.

Words of anger,

Now I'm a stranger.

Caught in this game,

Things will never be the same.

SANITY

Maybe I am crazy,

Maybe you should save me.

Tell me, what is sanity?

So I know what I shouldn't be,

People begging on the streets.

And you think you are bettering,

What you think that we should see,

What makes you different than me?

TRUTH

Your absence inspires me more than your presence,

Your depression rains down, you feign happiness.

What is it that you want from life?

Struggling just to make it through the nights.

USED TO

Used to say,

Good morning.

When I'd say goodnight,

Now I say good-bye.

THE SHINING

His personality is alright,

Shining so bright.

Illuminating me,

Setting me free.

BLUFF

Confounded, astounded;

How it was; how it is.

Never pictured life like this,

The beauty of not knowing.

Your truth is now showing,

Too broken to utter a stutter,

Too weak to give it up.

Was it worth it to call you bluff?

On a pier of self-denial,

Pick up the bottle; spill your bible.

In the end, you own your hurt.

It was you who threw the stones first.

GO

I let you go,

Pushed when I wanted,

You to stay.

I said goodbye,

Struggled back tears to send,

When I wanted you to ask why?

So I could say,

I love you too much,

Forever, tomorrow, yesterday, today.

SOMBER

And if it's time to say goodbye,

I hope you know,

These were the best years of my life.

Sorry I couldn't show,

How much I tried,

To make this right.

You're not mine to hold,

But I know we will be alright.

PERFECT

Tried to make me promise,

Never to fall for you.

Looking into your eyes,

As though you could do no wrong,

You played the perfect role.

In this fucked up fairytale,

Hidden well, within your web of lies.

Never thought you'd be the one,

Who would lead me to demise?

STATIC

Mentally,

I dig your grave.

Watch you suffocate,

In all the shit that you gave.

Physically,

I wait.

JOKER

Thought you could do it all,

Up and leave a mom.

Walk back after a decade,

A joke.

I'll throw some shade,

You were the waste of a phase.

WASTELAND

Never wanted to love you less,

Than today.

Every moment in association.

A waste.

NEEDFUL

Ashes blowing in the wind,

Life is a battle,

Everyone loses in the end.

Sometimes,

It is what it seems,

You don't always get what you need.

MOMMY

I know that you miss how it used to be,

With me, you, and mommy.

Playing games, being a family;

Daddy, it'll be alright.

I still love you,

Even though mommy is gone,

Believe in me.

I know she still loves us,

It will take some time,

Daddy please don't cry.

-not about my mom

EVERYTHING FALLS

Go on smiling,

As if nothing is wrong.

Isn't it hard to be so strong?

Everyone watching you,

Imitating your every move.

Like the shadows on your walls,

When things seem right,

Everything falls.

Crumbling in front of your eyes,

Trying hard not to give in to their lies.

THE REQUEIM

I'd live to die with you,

I'd die to be with you.

In the lands of eternal dreams;

Where I will finally be with you,

You let me live,

I let you die.

You took me by the hand,

I wish I never lived.

Hurt you with my lie,

In life, you cried for me,

In death, I answer you.

SONET

Secrets untold,

The world will never know.

The girl that hides within the shadows,

The girl that died alone.

They listened as she cried,

Watched the tears fall from her eyes,

She had no one to confide in,

In the faces of strangers, she lies.

Trust wasn't something she could deal with,

Hiding in the shadows,

She watches them smile.

Was her life even worthwhile?

When she goes home,

No one greets her,

All they do is mock and beat her.

We're not all the same,

Different people; different pain.

Finally, she runs away.

Even the angels cried for her that day.

DADDY

As you lay there,

In your bed,

You will always be,

My dad long dead.

I love you for who you are,

Not ever who you were,

Long before the scars and bruises.

I know what the truth is,

It was alcohol,

A heartless killer.

Deep down, you long to die;

For hurting that baby girl.

Your world,

Daddy I am different now.

I wanted you to know,

Daddy, I still love you.

And pray for you today.

-NOT ABOUT MY DAD

CORRUPT

I hear the calling,

My sweet addiction.

My way of solving,

What dulls the pain.

Wind through my hair;

The rush of the crowds,

No longer playing around.

Thirsty for the moment,

You see,

I will be,

Your sweet addiction.

OCEANIC BALLAD

Ocean point of view,

You cry out;

Cry out,

To the water.

Wanting someone to just hear you,

Wishing for someone to care,

Let the waters take you away.

To your own place,

Dancing waves will calm you,

The sun will set.

Reflections shimmering,

Upon that water in the beauty,

Of your eyes.

THAT GIRL

Can't stop thinking,

Who I want to be?

What I want to change (about me),

To be that girl.

Every time I feel so close,

I push them back away.

The ones who care,

That mean the most,

He'll never know.

Just can't tell him,

Whispering those words,

In her ears alone,

I will never be that girl.

THE STORY

I once asked a man,
As he lay there on his deathbed,
What he regrets most in life.
I will never forget his reply,
"it's funny you should ask,
That one question with a mask"
I ponder a moment;
Waiting for more.
"You see, my friend
It's the little things in life.
I loved that girl,
Couldn't say it,
No matter how I tried.
I loved her hair
And her beautiful eyes.
The way her smile,
Made waiting worthwhile.
Her laughter could ease my pain,
And clear away life's rain.
Never understood why,
I killed her with just one lie.
Oh what I would give,

To see her again."

NEVER DID

There is something,

That I think you should know.

I don't love you,

I never did.

I don't miss you,

Not even a bit.

I don't need you,

I have fallen again.

For myself,

And now,

I am unstoppable.

HOLLOW

I look at you,

No, through you.

Not like a person,

A mistake,

A shape,

A hollow shell;

Of a man,

Who isn't on my plain.

My existence,

Is not the same.

Acceptance

DESPERATE

If only,

Another man,

Could erase,

Every mark,

That you left on me.

Your strongest,

Was deceit.

NIHILITY

Your obsessions are your downfall;

Destroying sanity,

Replaced by vanity.

You'll have your way,

Then you're done;

Wither away,

Into the nihility,

You have made.

FALLEN

What have we become?

Trading places,

How low we've come.

How far we've gone,

Just a taste of fame,

Granted a moment of grace.

Just had to lost it all,

But who will be there,

When we begin to fall?

THE QUESTION

What if,

He loved you;

More than you did,

What then?

GAME TIME

Can you play the game?

Keep a straight face,

Walk away,

When you want to stay.

Can you play the game?

Leave all emotion,

No such thing as devotion.

Can you point blame?

When you try to play the game.

2:58 AM

Even when he holds me,

Touches me,

Runs his hands,

Down my body.

He is never,

You.

AWAKE

A whole night,

Even the very moment,

We reach the limits;

Is never enough,

To undo our past.

FADING

Silently suffering, falling so fast;

Losing all face,

Lost in the moment, faded in the masses.

The world is spinning so fast,

The food comes back up.

Losing the appetite, this is how it's meant to be;

So sustenance to keep you going, no strength, no drive.

Yearning for such vanity,

Wanting their beauty, their pride for yourself;

Screams echo; you are fat, ugly, and dumb,

Haunting your every move.

Get ready for the breakdown, everyone's watching now.

No tears left to cry,

No escape, nowhere left to hide;

Looking into the mirror,

"you're just useless"

"you'll never make it"

Listen closely, take a deep breath.

You're more than this,

You're a queen while they are playing make believe,

Keep thriving, keep surviving.

You'll live in a world of your own creation.

There's more to life than cheap tricks and short-lived vanity.

REFLECT

Time has failed us,

Reflections as we gaze into the water,

Taking in what we let go.

As time flies by,

Like water, let it flow;

Never looking back again,

What could have been?

What never happened?

Dreaming of the past,

We must let go; we must let go.

If you could go back,

Change all that didn't go our way,

Such selfish acts.

We wouldn't be the same,

Lessons learned,

Mistakes are made.

Reflections of who we were,

Who we've been.

There is always shame,

Don't let it guide us anymore.

Live to learn,

Learn to live.

THE CHASE

I see the future in your eyes,

Joy is made from taking chances.

To hold and cherish until I die,

My love grows, like trees with their branches.

Season always due to turn,

I will stand forever by your side,

Like the rosy hues of the leaves, my passion will always burn.

In bad times, you were my safe place to hide;

Forever and always, that's what they say.

From the end to beginning,

I'll love you yesterday, tomorrow, today.

We are un-ending,

Love (the chase).

LOVE

Knees grow weak-

Heart beats faster,

Can hardly breathe,

Can feel the pitter patter,

Yearning for such passion.

The look in your eyes,

Warm and soft,

Oh so loving.

A smile on that face-

Makes me feel better,

Makes me break,

Bursting with love,

It must be fate!

Sweet music is made,

With each word you speak,

So much more to hear,

Without even a peep.

Perfect creation,

Divine devotion,

Alas, you are quintessential;

Love.

THE DIFFERENCE

Sometimes,

I love it when a worthy romance will die.

The essence of what was real-

Helps me to survive,

Makes me grow and thrive,

The days, so much filth.

Like the words pouring from your mouth,

Vile sewage,

Warps and devours,

Leaving all around you without.

And still;

I live for the next tomorrow,

Cease of lust and passions,

Leaving me content, with no such sorrows.

To be completely honest,

I could care less to see you again,

A soulless, deteriorating carnage;

Not even reminisced as friend.

ANOTHER CHAPTER

Like the ghost of Christmas past;

You hold on, to make it last.

Found at the point of no return,

A chapter written,

Another lesson that's never learned.

GAMES

You're so caught up in your games-
Losing so much, you're to blame.
The fights and the stupid shit,
Tell me, in the end was it worth it?
You know how it will end,
Hope for the best, no regrets; you can't pretend.
The mind games are your devices,
So that you can survive this,
And I watch as you play again.
How foolish of me, I thought you were a friend;
I don't want to watch you fall apart,
Won't be played again, as I was from the start.
What really matters to you?
How much more will you go through?
Before you break under the pressure,
Too proud to admit that you don't want to lose her,
You'll drive yourself insane,
Keep living for these games.
And if you decide that you're enough,
I'll be there when it gets rough,
Quite playing games, enough is enough.

NEVER SAY NEVER

Said you'd never leave-
Always have my back,
Inconsistent inconvenience,
Too late now.
Damage has gone rampant,
Pain is numbed down,
Dumbing down the masses,
Coping, I hope it lasts.
Whittling down your soul,
What's left, that mind;
Stronger than you know.
The pain, let it go;
Just another echo,
I let you go,
Hands behind my back.
Twisted ego,
Took beauty from within the best,
Memory at best,
There is nothing left.

HI

And all I wanted to do was say hi,

Not sorry, no inquiries, hi.

I know it in my stomach,

This isn't going to change us,

But I can't get the words out,

I miss you, I'm happy now.

I miss you; you'll knock them out,

Meant to be, what's that mean;

Can it be?

Nothing is really as it seems,

I'm sorry,

But I'm not.

I'm hurting,

But I'm strong.

Pride, hardwired in our brains;

To make us act this way,

Be safe, be astounding in your ways,

Never forget, there are always better days.

STAY

If it will make you stay,

Then stay.

But I won't do it-

Not today,

Not ever.

Piss off, just go;

Guess what I am trying to say is,

BUH BYE!

Enjoy your day!

ACCEPTANCE

Accept that you're angry,

Or sad or disappointed,

Accept that it happened.

And let it go, just breathe;

Denial grows pestilent, now apathy,

When it happens,

You're just like them.

SO MUCH

Dear anxiety,

Why do you take my sleep?

It means so much to me,

When you let me dream!

THE NUMBING

How do you numb the pain?

Or do you feel at all?

How do you play this game?

Drink till you stumble and crawl;

Covering your issues,

Drowning them down,

When you wake,

It's back in your face.

How many more nights to run?

Just to carry it with the sun.

SO GREAT

You asked me to wait for you-

Said we would be great,

So great,

Why should I wait?

When you should have stayed (you),

I don't deal with maybes,

I'd give it one last try,

Just not tonight.

VOW

You'll never know-

What you have lost,

When you said,

Goodbye.

FOREVER

You are,

And will forever be,

The most imperfect thing,

That I will never need.

ALMOST WON

On my level-

They don't understand,

Try to bring me down,

For a moment.

Almost won,

You'll never,

Be on my level,

If you can't ever,

Be,

Okay.

THAT WAY

I love you-

Not in that way.

You'll understand,

One day.

Feigning ignorance,

Is not the way to bliss.

LINGERING

Thoughts always linger-

On what I should have done.

Could have told you everything;

Things aren't always what they seem,

How can I trust you?

I don't even trust myself.

TO THE MOON

Ride or die;

Baby, you'd just run and hide.

Basically you're a want-to-be,

Parading around like you're better,

You only wish you were me.

To the moon and back,

Unaware, I am everything that you lack.

CONSUMING

Consumed by the flames-

Burning from your claims,

You've been forsaken,

Judge me? Surely, you're mistaken.

Chew you up and spit you out,

This world, it's mine now.

TRUTH HURTS

You seem happy now-

How sad.

That it still comes from,

A bottle…

PRAYERS

I prayed that you would,

Never leave.

And hoped you wouldn't forget,

The nights that we spent,

Just you and me.

It's much too late now,

For regret.

Thank You

DIVINATION

You must be on the fast track to the divine;

Effortlessly, you're leaving footprints in my mind.

A hindrance, depravity from all effervescent radiance,

Shattering the hourglass, stealing away the time.

Unknown, such a blessing in disguise;

Breaking free, chasing shadows from my dreams.

Coming clean, ones ridden with such doubt;

Now shining with pure beauty.

Opening my mind,

Accepting everything as a blank new page.

You change this in me,

Like a beast set free from the cage.

Untamable, uncalmable, unrestricted by human designs,

Free to roam and free to fly.

THE STORY

When the world has its way of telling,
A beautiful story or a Hollywood horror.
When pens and needles fall to the ground;
Yet never make a sound,
Only then, will you be forgotten.
An angel perfectly made,
Reminiscing on your sweet face,
The words never spoken to me,
Wishing that you'd never leave.
I miss you more each day,
Always there to keep me going,
In a harsh world, you're the greatest friend;
Always remembered, until we meet again…

ONE DAY

One day, you'll want someone to hold onto;

One day, there will be someone worth my time.

To catch me when I fall,

To be there through it all,

So why waste more time?

They say love is blind,

You're so great at deceit,

But I know, you're no good for me.

LOST IT

The way that you go through life,

Never knowing where you're headed.

No real emotion,

Heart still beats, but the feeling is dead;

So one day I hope that you'll see,

How much better off you could be,

You had a chance at everything,

You lost it.

MINE

He's beautifully made;

Perfectly defined,

A gentle soul,

So thankful,

That he's mine.

FLINGS AND THINGS

Someday you won't mean a thing;

Just a dusty memory of some fling.

Not worth the time or emotion spent,

You'll be alone, wondering where the days went.

We all get older, move on with our lives;

Someday having families, be husbands and wives,

Blessed by joy as the dark clouds fade,

Watching in the sidelines, you'll wish you had stayed.

YOURS

Hold me now;

And show me,

How forever feels,

For I am,

Eternally yours.

VISUALIZE

When the sun goes down-

I'll keep my eyes closed,

Visualize,

The way you hold me.

How perfect our life,

Could be,

Would be,

Is,

Here in this moment.

YOUR WAYS

So strong-

So brave,

You're so perfect.

In all your ways,

Love sharing with you,

All the good times,

Of our lives.

QUEEN

I oft find myself within a vivid daydream;

Vibrant hues, and all that's good surrounds me.

For one moment I had it all, queen.

I found everything when you held me,

I could see emotion in your eyes,

A subtle passion building when you were near.

And like everything else, feelings too must die;

I may have let go, but at least I tried.

DIFFERENCE

You're not like the others;

Different vibes,

Different auras,

Intriguing to say,

The least.

STARS

I want to lie under the stars;

Let's talk about these scars.

Reminiscing on the greater days,

Before life leaves and memories fade,

Let's take a good long walk,

Gaze upon those effervescent landscapes, let's talk.

Laugh until we can hardly breathe;

Make memories of you and me.

MOVE ON

Addicted to your afflictions;

Burdens of your own device,

Move on,

Bye!

TOYS

Maybe-

You'll give her joy.

Or maybe,

Like me,

She is just another toy.

To toss,

Once you've broken,

Her,

You're nothing;

But a spoiled little boy.

WISE MAN

A wise man said-

Let it go.

A wise man said-

Pick your battles, it's your war.

A wise man said-

He isn't worth it,

Set your boundaries.

A wise man said-

Fuck what they think.

A wise man said-

Maybe it's best to walk away,

Maybe a wise man, is in my head.

SELF-SACRIFICE

Forever and always;

I'll have your back.

But only when I can,

When convenient,

Fuck that.

You're crazy,

I'll keep mine,

Bye now, self-sacrifice.

BRAVO!

And you said that you're not like them;

You said you don't have to prove or impress.

You did,

Here's your standing ovation;

Congratulations.

A minute made creation, your salvation.

Off you go; you mindless clone,

Sold your soul, to the screen of a phone.

Bravo!

JUST THERE

When you're high, you don't care;

When you're drunk, you don't either.

Pure amusement is all;

When you're sober, no one's there.

Basically you're an idiom;

Useless, not priceless, just there.

Maybe they get high off you;

A couple of laughs, bemused.

Then you're nothing again, nothing at all;

Destroyed by drugs and a broken ego.

APATHY

Who would have thought?

You,

Inspired me by apathy.

Meaningless, in a sense;

I'll be off now,

Recompense,

Does it even matter now?

STRONG

You said it's lonely, being strong;

It's not.

It's lonelier to be strung along;

By someone selfish like you.

LIFE AND GOODBYES

I saw a picture of you yesterday;

And again, felt joy and strength,

As soon as I closed my eyes,

Then comes the rain.

Breaking all over;

I never got to say goodbye.

I'll love you forever and always,

Everything happens for a reason,

Everything in the universe is foretold.

I wish you didn't have to leave so soon,

I still miss you.

LET'S TALK

Talk is cheap;

Dirt cheap.

Show me the action

Behind the lies

THE TRUTH

As if words were enough;
To make me stay.
Actions are proof, even in denial-
That even seasoned liars can't control,
You can't provoke the beast,
And stroke the ego,
To walk away unscathed.
You've made yourself a fool,
Even that mirror cracks,
Instead of giving in to you,
Black veils swallow all light,
As you enter a room.
Because the one thing you can't hide,
Is the truth.

2:00 AM

So glad that it happened;

When you said hi.

Walked into my life,

Such wonderous events,

Plot twists and developments.

You shine joy, kill all sadness;

Knowledge and patience,

Truly a blessing, heaven sent.

A MOMENT

I wish that I could make you feel-

How dead you make me.

No taste to the tongue,

Just a seeming less ritual,

To pass a moment,

Or two.

GREAT THINGS

Great things are happening-

You drink yourself to sleep.

Great things are happening-

You get high just to get by.

Great things are happening-

I'm right and you are wrong.

Great things are happening-

I report you thinking I am strong.

Great things, they are happening-

As I wave my goodbyes.

Great things are happening-

As I let go of your song.

NO MORE

No more games-

No more,

No more lies-

No more,

A fantasy world;

That's all yours.

No more time,

Waiting for your sanity,

You're slipping, you see-

You

Have

Sank.

I hope you know,

That it's too late.

NEVER DO

Thank you-

For all those things

You would never do.

Never laugh,

Never smile,

Now I am living.

From all those things,

You would never do.

STOLE THE ROLE

Don't forget-

This is your fault

I grow stronger

As you fall.

In your own ways;

You victimized me,

Stole the role,

Sorry baby.

I don't take supporting actor;

Move along,

Just don't ever forget,

This is your place.

MUST BE NICE

Living in your fantasy-

Must be nice,

Telling them you took care of me,

And our child.

You see-

It's nice to run away,

Come back and try to take,

Everything,

That you could never have.

On our own;

A happy life,

A healthy smile,

Without you.

Yet you're still claiming-

To be the one providing,

When you can't even sleep,

In your own home.

No one to confide in,

You lash out,

You're in the past now,

Living in the moment,

Loving the path that I have chosen.

BETTER OR WORSE

Without you-

Pictures on my walls,

Remind me of how things used to be.

Realizing now; I'm changed,

For better or worse,

You once stood beside me.

Unbreakable pillar,

Holding me up,

So strong.

Where are you now?

Depressions darkest hour;

Horrors of my mind,

Break me down,

Where did you go?

When I needed you the most?

ONCE

What once was-

Feeble hearts shatter,

Souls once calm and collected,

Filled with rage until enflamed.

A world with chains that bind you;

Unknowing, unwilling; hiding in the shadows,

Gazing at unfamiliar faces,

Suffocating,

What once was, will never be.

A MOCKERY

Your beauty mocks me-

Death cold lips and pale skin,

Growing more desolate each day,

Basking in the glory that I once was.

I will return,

Revenge, driven by hate;

It's too late,

Writhing in me, it will never die.

From all the times you deceived me,

Stole my life,

A rose red with stains,

For love through the pain.

The most beautiful angel of death,

I will love you through the hate.

X

JM

I can't do this anymore-

Failed to find inspiration,

Other than pain, disappointment, and depression.

I'd give up the rest of my life,

For one more day with you.

JM

Be Still My Soul

FOOTPRINTS

Little footprints on the floor-

From my staircase,

To the bedroom door.

Little footprints,

In the hallway,

In each room.

Little footprints,

Leading me to everything,

That I will ever need.

MY HEART!!!

Be still my heart!

So perfect, so smart!

Little hands, a giant smile;

My heart is in the eyes of my child!

PARENTHOOD

Into the madness-

We go.

Holding hands,

Inseparable bonds,

Keep each other safe.

We stay humble,

Mother and son.

CHILD

Small and wise-

They grow independent.

Strong and agile,

Steady their ground,

Curious and learning,

Little wheels turning,

The world,

Of a child.

STRENGTH OVER DIGNITY

I must be strong-

For them today

I must be strong.

Because they're afraid,

Because you walked away,

I made myself strong,

I am unafraid.

To keep them safe,

From their darkest days.

NO WRONG

Everything else aside-

I held it all inside.

Must be strong,

Because-

To them I can do no wrong.

SONG

Rain creates song,

With each drop,

Fallen.

Whistles of the wind,

Create harmony,

Mind wanders into,

This peaceful serene.

A place of pure magic;

Gazing-

Into that mirror,

To see-

What matters most.

Happiness-

Is in the eye of the beholder.

So vivacious and majestic,

Clearing-

My insecurities

All loneliness

Fades away.

As I stare-

Into the eyes

Of my children.

GREATEST GIFTS

A gift from the gods-

Small and mighty

Both scared

And brave.

Curious-

And finding.

The greatest gift-

Little feet

Made to carry.

Little hands-

To hold.

So bright-

And so loving

The true meaning

Of a blessed life.

NO SOUNDS

When the sun goes down-

And no one is around,

There are no sounds.

No fireflies to dance around,

No children running wild,

No one knows that child.

No one calls his name,

Or holds his hand,

May his soul rest in peace,

I will always love that boy.

EVERY MOVE

I can't stand it anymore-
Waiting and watching,
Every move made,
Acting like I'm afraid.
I could tell you everything-
In my mind you already know,
It's not so complicated,
I can't let it show.
I am weaker than you,
On day
It may be too late,
I'll tell you everything,
To make you stay.
Everyone closest to me-
I push away,
Can't find the strength to say.
What I really mean,
Maybe you'll be mine one day.

LOVE FOR ME

A heart in the trees-

Makes me weak,

In the knees,

As I know now,

Even the wind blows,

That even when the moon recedes,

There is still a love for me.

FELT YOU

I felt you again-

So warm and soft.

I held your hand-

I thought you were lost.

HEADSTRONG

A sweet laugh-

Innocent smile,

Enchanting eyes,

A thousand freckles.

Blessed on his face-

Headstrong, brilliant in mind,

I can't believe that you are mine.

Ten creeps up quickly,

You handsome,

Amazing,

Mini me!

JUST ONE MORE

Just one more-

Innocent cheeked kiss.

Just one more-

Good night hug.

Just one more-

Story before you slumber.

Just another-

Tear before you're off.

Just one more moment-

While you're young.

Just one more-

Beautiful smile,

My child.

Break the Chains

WILDFIRE

Those eyes that shine so bright,

Much hope, because sorrow is for yesterday.

Break free from your chains,

No limits, just unending light.

Echoes of the past cannot shatter the future.

When you let go of hesitation,

And set free your burning passions.

Let it rage like a wildfire,

For those are brighter days,

That shine within those eyes.

THE BLIND

Blind leading blind-

When will they realize?

Truth is in each of them;

We are living,

In a controlled,

Subconscious cage.

TIME

The master of everything,

No end and no beginning.

Making you feel light and airy as a released spring.

Or weighed down, burdened, and strained,

It can make all wounds heal,

Create towers and wither away the seas.

Numb away you pain or change your feelings completely.

Fervent yet apathetic, everything in between.

Reminiscing- illuminating the joys and all the sorrows,

Gone within the blink of an eye, or lasting a lifetime,

Our ally for all our tomorrows,

And the greatest enemy for all that follows,

Time.

BEGIN AGAIN

First wreck, train-wreck;

Twenty-seven years old.

Emotions welling,

Can't stop, don't stop.

People love you; you know.

This isn't the end,

Begin again,

Love yourself.

CHOICES

Wake up-

Eyes wide open.

Wake up-

You're still frozen.

Stand up-

Or do you even have a voice?

Sleep now-

It's your choice.

PERPLEX

A blank page-

What's next?

Stare for a moment-

Perplexed!

Astounding emotion-

Write it down!

A pile of scribbles-

You have found!

Hope you like it,

I don't even know,

But it's time for me to go!

SACRIFICE

I don't believe in sacrifice;

No YOUS, MEs, OR I's.

We all deserve life,

Somehow; out of mind, out of sight.

100

If it means 100 lies;

To rid you of you disguise,

I will fight,

Until the wrongs are right.

WISHING

I'd love to be a Disney Princess;

Only, I don't have the breasts!

Should I go for surgery?

Or merely settle for me?

Play the game,

Or stay the same,

Walk the line,

Or be the blind?

Hollywood hysteria,

Or media criteria,

If you want,

I'll change the font.

But you'll still see,

I'm me.

LET GO

All that matters; is now,

Today.

Don't live for tomorrows-

Let go of

Yesterday.

YOU SEE

A miracle, blessing, and curse;

You decide what is worse,

Harmony turns to tragedy,

It is all in how you see.

2018

Dear 2018-

It's about time,

That I swallowed my pride,

I've done so much wrong.

I thought I was being strong,

In the end; it will be alright,

Because I grew in this fight.

Not a yearlong battle,

But a lifelong journey.

Time to get back onto the saddle,

This is not the end,

I'll keep living and learning.

I miss you; I am yearning;

For the touch that's gone away,

But the memories remain.

Growing from the lessons,

Thankful for the blessings,

It's not a year of loss.

A chapter of knowledge,

Learning who I am.

I am more than just a woman.

Breathe

You are amazing-

You are not a victim,

Don't pretend to be,

In the end; you pick your battles.

Win or lose, that's on you.

Decide now; what is your mentality?

Be what you want to be,

Just don't stay there long,

You must be strong.

Your actions dictate your mind;

Your mind dictates your actions,

Live happy, live great, and grow,

Or at least give a good show!

Smile; it's effortless,

Yet overwhelmingly warm,

If it's loss, smile, you'll earn more.

Love is limitless when you open the door,

Don't lower your standards,

By gods don't you settle.

But don't be upset,

If you choose to meddle,

Petty games are for children,

Now it's your turn; lose or win?

SHUTTLE

A whole new level;

While you're in so much shit,

Might need a shovel,

While I'm blasting off,

In a space shuttle.

RULES

We've gone as far as we can-

Breaking rules

And all the lies.

Is it still even worth it to try?

To try?

EVERYONE ELSE

Everyone is watching-

Thinking that they know me.

Hiding behind the mask-

Thinking that I am happy.

But nothing,

Nothing is ever what it seems.

There's more to me,

Than what you have seen.

OUR TIME

Frozen; a moment in time-

When everything is alright.

We gave up our will to try,

Here, right now.

Life is at a standstill,

Take our time,

Figure out what really matters (to you).

UNTIL I DIE

What will become of me?

Will I die bitter and lonely?

Secrets held deep inside,

Keeping them safe, until I die.

IN THREES

The rain won't stop-

Beating down,

On this cold and shattered heart.

Loneliness creeping in,

Like shadows on the walls,

Hearing those words again,

As lighting streaks across the skies.

LOST

I am lost;

In the maze of my mind.

Reality and fantasy intertwined.

Sanity is so hard to find,

No one here, save for me.

BLINK

Life can change-

With the blink of an eye,

Peace can end and war arise.

Take a long and hard look,

Is this what you wanted?

Creator

ULTIMATE REACTION

STOP

Listen to the echoes of your soul;

You are far stronger than you'll ever know.

BREATHE

Take a moment to contemplate your truth;

Let each moment reflect your youth.

LISTEN

To all the stories of your past;

A lesson learned, as nothing is made to last.

CONTEMPLATE

On the reality of your depravity;

Releasing the tension, you're now in zero gravity.

RELEASE

All the materialistic possessions;

You're worth more than your vain obsessions.

FEEL

All the emotions lifting away;

As there is simply no day; no day like today.

FREE YOURSELF

From this non-existent plain;

You have not lived in vain.

STOP

Face to face, with your own reflection;

You've come to the ultimate reaction.

MISTAKEN

My life is not like yours;

We are nothing alike,

Your silver spoon and I struggle.

Your pampered nights,

My life is not like yours,

Never given, never easy.

Always striving for success,

Starving, hungry for the best.

Ungrateful, you scoff and scorn;

Your reality is torn,

In sudden retrospect;

We've been mistaken,

My life is much like yours.

Two views,

Different sides, but the same coin

Imagine love,

If our views were joined.

THE CREATOR

The walls are caving in-

Can't move, can't breathe.

In the distance, there's a solemn light.

Fight or flight;

Used, ridiculed, paralyzed by this damned reality.

And the truth is just a disease you see,

In a world based on small decisions.

I bleed out the fear, this is my vision,

Ease the tension, focus on the moment.

Life is a bitch, don't know it until you blow it,

Take a second, free your focus.

It all comes to now, and you had better own it;

Everyone's looking now, waiting for your failure.

In this moment, you're the creator.

Seize it, rise and meet your maker!

IN A DREAM

Trivial pursuit-

Chase happy or just be?

How complex your life must seem?

If you're only well in a dream.

MOTIONS

Going through the motions-

Day in, day out.

On your phone,

In your zone,

Zombie of the mass media.

A slave in your own game,

Wake up, wake up;

Or is this your destiny?

An apocalypse of your mind,

Your own demise,

You are fiction.

REFRACTION

A look into the mirror-

It's clear,

Not clearer,

You're a reflection on the glass.

Refracting not reflecting,

The future, present, the past.

MY COMFORT

You warm my soul-

Comfort me,

A blanked of love,

Give me energy.

Always there,

On time,

Oh how I love you,

Coffee, my comfort.

NOT YOU

I wait for no one-

I need no-one but me.

My actions, my emotions;

I love it,

Not you.

CREATOR

I am a creator-

My life, my story.

Saw you walk away,

You'll come back today,

Remorse is a strong emotion.

I have depth, like an ocean;

Not tidal waves, a tsunami

And you'll come running back to me.

THE LASH

I've built empires on your absence-

Miss you, but I don't.

Strange isn't it?

Setting boundaries,

I set out to show you my pain;

Must have hurt,

Because

You RAN AWAY.

Leaving me, hurt;

But pain goes away,

And that's how empires are made.

NAKED

Standing here naked-

Emotionally out in the open,

Which path do you choose?

Confront the issues or run away;

Show your character proudly.

A BIT MORE LOVE

Love like someone you loved-

Love like someone you never lost,

Love those that walked away,

Loved those that are here today.

Love yourself until you find

Your pieces,

Love your emotions,

They have their reasons.

Because this world only needs-

Just a bit more love.

HUMANLY

Maybe I should have settled-

And never meddled,

In such humanly affairs.

DECISIONS, DECISIONS

Decide now-

What you want.

Decide then-

Where you want to be.

Win or lose,

It's up to you.

Just remember,

I'll always have your back,

I will always love you.

COBRA

Put your crown on-

Upside down

Lay around.

On a throne-

That's made of bones,

Constricted,

Your prey.

Hesitation,

No sounds,

In your wake.

The bones, they do break;

In the eyes

Of a snake.

ARISE

In the eyes of a madman;

You are obscene.

In the eyes of a sad man;

You are a queen.

THE GIVING

Faith, you see-

Is nothing more,

Than self-love,

And giving some more.

YOUR MOMENT

Don't lose sight-

Your goals, they're obtainable;

They can't see it,

You're unstoppable.

See yourself there,

And realize,

Everything is right,

Seize your moment!

TURNING

Drip drop-

Of a coffee pot.

It's four AM;

And the world keeps on turning,

Not in the city lights anymore,

Not waiting for laughter,

Through-

That door.

Pristine lights aglow in the distance,

But now you're in the path,

To least resistance.

Goals are made,

Dates are set,

Your pockets,

Lighter.

Girl, you're a fighter;

From a small town,

You are city bound,

Again and again.

Break the cycle,

Set your mold,

You're golden, girl.

WHAT'S REAL?

Sometimes the hardest part-

Is letting go,

But holding on,

You'll never grow.

Deciphering lies from truth,

Honestly, what's real to you?

GLORY

As the sun rises,

Trees dance,

Calmly.

Surreal, pure beauty;

Nature in its glory.

STEP ASIDE

I made it through-

The dark;

Now I'm creating,

A glorious work of art.

Step aside,

The time for you has died.

IRRELEVENT

Don't get it twisted-

You've been mis-fitted;

Used, irrelevant, replaced.

Time to learn your place,

I'm going places.

Creating new lands;

You're stuck in the sands,

Of your lies,

And made up faces.

CREATIONS

Off in time and space-

I define this place.

Creating reality-

Beauty as far

As the eye can see.

THE FLAWS

Growth isn't always easy-

Acknowledging

Self-flaws

Without deceiving.

Letting go of all that holds,

Ascending the stars,

A new story must be told.

I AM THE LIGHT

All eyes on me-

Try as you might.

I was created,

To be a creator.

I was designed,

To succeed.

I am the light.

NEW

Brand new-

Broke the mold.

Brand new-

While you sit down,

Outdated;

Brand new,

And I'm breaking all the limits.

MOTHER E

You cannot take-

What was never meant to be yours.

You cannot break-

What never belonged (to you).

You cannot fake-

What your beating heart desires.

You cannot smother-

A soul that burns as fire.

You cannot shatter to pieces-

Mother Earth's sovereign love.

PUZZLING

Nothing but riddled words-

Scribbles of nonsense on paper,

Before me.

It's not until you learn the meaning,

Of what it's like to be free;

-puzzling, isn't it?

NIGHT

A coolness in my soul-

Like a stream in the mountains,

Dew drops basked with the sun,

Velvet skies of morning.

I want to soak it in;

Until the world goes silent,

As the night.

YOUR OWN LOVE

Love yourself first-

And then one more time.

Love yourself more-

And you will be fine.

Others are passing;

Some more slow,

But with your own love,

You will forever grow.

THE BOLD

It is never too late-

To change the tides of fate.

Behold the light unto you,

Boost your weary soul,

As fortune favors the bold.

BLISSFUL

A grateful heart-

And blissful soul;

Brings abundance onto you,

Seek now and you shall hold.

MY BODY

My body-

Simply is my body.

My body, dear-

Is flawed

Is wounded

Is human.

My body-

Is my temple

Is sacred

Is powerful

Is mine.

My body-

Is a creator

Is glorious

Is divine.

MY MIND

My mind-

Is one of a kind.

Hardwired and accurately designed,

To create misery and sadness,

Happiness and madness.

My mind-

Is in its own; divine.

Powerful and potent,

A whole world resides,

In the space of my mind.

Destiny

Detachment from reality,
Don't get attached easily.
Obsessed with shear vanity,
This is my reality.
Full of false pretenses,
You've grown so pretentious.
When the curtains come down,
In mutiny, you will drown.
Vicious abnormalities,
Life won't get the best of me,
Gaze upon the reflection, just breathe.
There is a monster hidden beneath,
Let it out, set it free;
For the world isn't ready for its destiny.

SOMETIMES

Sometimes-

I just don't know about me.

Sometimes-

What you get is what you see.

Sometimes-

I contemplate many choices.

Sometimes-

My thoughts have many voices.

Sometimes-

I lower my values, my standards.

Because sometimes-

I just need to feel accepted,

Just need to feel "love"

CASUALTIES OF THE WORLD

Soul inside is set aflame,

Living a life of shame.

As I see it, my world is different than yours,

What are we living for? Fighting, breathing, and dying for?

A thousand miles away, there is a war;

Here, there is a war merely to feed the poor.

What image must be given to others?

Where so often the rich get by, while others suffer.

This war echoes far,

Harming more than just soldiers.

There is more pain than physical harm,

Our minds become weaker; hearts grow colder.

Everyone is fighting this battle,

More people on the streets fading away.

Not casualties of this war,

Casualties of the world.

YOUR DESTINY

What is true?

What's seen and what's heard,

Unbeknownst, the programming;

Unwilling to believe,

You've always held the key,

To your destiny.

OUR GLORY

An undelivered message could cost a war,

But looking back; they caused far more.

Insecurity breeds uncertainty, often leading to casualties;

What's wrong with today's society?

So quick to blame others;

Like children bickering with one another.

Things never seem to change with time.

Just repeating over and over as if a verse to rhyme,

Story is always the same.

Someone dies for another's fame,

As time goes by, re-watch the story;

A nation falls for another's glory,

Wouldn't it be nice if things were different?

If "great leaders" weren't so hell bent;

On nation into pieces,

All because they failed to listen.

AT PEACE

When I lay at peace with soul-

No burden is left to behold,

Once held the world upon my shoulders,

Prayed to never grow older.

Time flew by,

On silver wings of the falcons,

Body begins to ware down,

Why?

Why me?

To burden myself with the sins of humanity.

To weep for them when they don't cry;

To die for them, to save a soul.

If so many a star to fill the heavens,

Then why not, by the love of thy children;

Can't all the hearts of the world be mend?

DEAR REALITY

Music defines us;

No, our wardrobe does,

Our make-up,

Hair,

And beauty.

Based on waistlines-

Conformed

To socialized norms.

A truly unrealistic,

Un-idealistic reality.

DIRECTIONS

Up or down;

East or west.

Choose a path,

Open your eyes.

Your destiny;

One step at a time,

MEANT FOR

Rise above the masses;

Keep pushing-

Thriving

You're meant for more,

Than miniscule ideals.

UNREQUITED

And all that remains are the ill-fated stains,

My story is made as the ink flows through my veins.

Feet to guide, hands to find, yet deaf to the sight.

Maybe one day, I may gaze upon the voice of light,

Fear subsides, as insanity has no equal.

Soul stained pages, a book with no sequel.

Where the rest of me, sands of time vanquished,

Never did I know, that it would go like this.

In the dark I'm blind, searching for mere echoes,

A paradox; the truth that no one knows.

Some clarity, only understood by the maddest of men.

You decide now, the only certainty is how you choose it to end.

THE PRESSURE

Be normal-

Be happy

How do I

Define such madness?

Society so full of pills,

A dumbing down,

Red makes you happy,

Blue makes you sane.

Come down, feel crappy;

One more should do,

Who said you had to die?

To be a zombie.

IN THE STARS

This time I won't write your name;

Inscribed in my soul,

You can never let it go.

Set it to flames,

This time it will sink in,

Our fate is written in the stars.

FREE

Freedom comes to those,

Who want it.

Spiritually, not physically;

As you cannot cage,

A soul that knows,

It-self.

DESIGNED

I am beautifully woven-

Of fear and courage,

I tread the line with caution.

Learning truths,

I grow defiant of norms,

You cannot stop me.

PLACES

She's going places,

But not with you.

She's moving mountains,

And finding truth.

Your words lack conviction,

She's equalizing with poetic diction.

Leaving you confounded,

She is more astounded,

Gained her grace so well,

It was only you who fell.

Like monkeys in a barrel,

Stay there, your madness is your hell.

THE LEAD

Follow me-

And I'll show you,

A world

Free of limitations.

MODESTY

Modesty-

Honestly

I don't know the meaning.

Kind of deceiving,

Just keep conceiving,

The idea, of idea, of a word.

Humble-

Wow, I'm so jumbled;

With emotions, controlled

With medication, it is consoled.

Bumbled rhymes with humble,

Are you bumbled to be humbled?

Or humbled to be bumbled?

That is a thing, right?

REAL LOVE

I won't break-

Under the pressure

Of finding love,

In a world

Built to destroy the idea.

UNDRESS TRUTH

My eyes-

Are green

My eyes-

Have seen

Children born,

Lovers die,

People unite.

My eyes-

Have witnessed,

Sacred ties,

Best friends fight,

Beauty subsides.

My eyes-

Will not water,

Will not faulter,

Because of goodbyes.

THE MOON

You are the sun to the moon;

And without you,

The stars don't shine as bright.

The feeling of heaven is uplifted,

Bringing storms upon my soul,

As all roses may have thorns.

Surely you know,

May you find peace,

Enough to rise about clouds of self-grief.

And find your happiness on top of a mountain,

Clear of rain.

Basking in rays of sun;

As I did, as I've done.

LET IT OUT

Time; so wonderfully daunting-

If memories keep haunting,

Your subconscious.

Write it down, they say;

Take a deep breath,

You've got this,

Let it all out now.

Ink flows like tears without sound,

One day, you too will have bliss.

THE QUESTIONS

Who is me?

Who am I?

Where are we?

Where are we going now?

THE NEEDS

What more could you want?

What more could you need?

Search within yourself now,

What battle do you choose to feed?

WILL BE

What is meant to be;

Will simply be.

The universe gives what we think;

So will you fly, or will you sink?

GO AWAY

I will smile-

For a while

What do you want?

GOLDEN

You are a god amongst men-

Driving them to sin

A god you say, commence.

What? Recompense?

My sins are my own;

The seeds, I have sown.

Regret, agony, and greed;

For me, myself, I will bleed.

THE DRUG

Letting go and moving on-

Funny, that's when it comes again.

The apology, withdrawal sets in;

A drug of the senses,

But alas, we all relapse.

THE MEASURES

How do you measure "love"?

Is it even real?

Like joy, sorrow, angst, and anger;

Or mere lust with added intentions.

Just like trust, respect, and dignity;

Only words we give our own meaning.

Is love nothing but an illusion?

Created by poets and the lonely,

To project purpose upon another.

Was it ever real? A means to an end?

Words without purpose even so,

Are merely just things lacking meaning.

In the end, it is just a word;

How do you measure something?

Of no value at all?!?

YOU DECIDE

How do you measure yourself?

Weight, height, ounces;

No, how do you measure YOU love?

Your character reflected or refracted;

Through your eyes or theirs?

Living a lie or for your truth;

Are you a feather?

Or an anchor?

Their views or your own,

A mirror is the soul of your eyes,

Are you carefree or limited?

Stressed or free,

What kind of life do you choose?

SOME PEOPLE

Some people will come to stay-
Some will walk away,
Some will smile,
Some will hate.
Some people will tell you things-
Some will be honest,
Some will make up stories,
Just to avoid reaction,
Some people will hold you close-
Some will push you away,
Some will build you up,
And tear you down,
Some will laugh with you,
Some at you.
Some people will be friends for life-
Some just for a day,
Some people promise forever,
Just so that they can play.
Some people will make you smile-
Some will break you down,
You are more than some people,
Yesterday, tomorrow, today.

Your word means more to some people,
You are stronger than some people,
Some need that in different ways.
No matter where you are in life,
Losing people, gained, lost, afraid;
You are special to some people.

JOURNEYS

The journey unwinding,
Inside and out.
The soul keeps echoing,
What's lost-
Can never be found,
A deep resonance of emotion,
Searching for a sound,
That makes a heart beat,
Proverbial footsteps,
That make the knees weak.
Such warmth is confounding,
To wake up and see,
To finally be free,
Of socialized norms.
A love so surreal,
Unleash; un-wield.
Such divine intervention,
To live in a moment.

OPEN DOORS

An open door-

Leads to nothing,

Leads to madness,

Leads to more.

An open door-

Shows a cure,

A blessing,

A curse.

An open door-

One more opportunity,

Just one more, open door.

HOLY FATHER

I want to show you-

The weak and weary,

The strength they show me.

I want to teach you-

The dumb and the feeble,

Oh, those lessons they teach me.

I want to hold you-

Oh those cold and shaking,

How they warm me.

I want to love you,

As I love those who can't.

HOME

I found home-

When I was leaving.

I found hope-

While I was bleeding.

I found love-

While I was retreating,

When faith was broken,

And options began to fade.

I found home,

In faith and believing.

A NEW KIND OF FREEDOM

A new freedom-

From old constrictions.

Endless opportunities-

From being abandoned.

True strength,

Is in gratitude.

Beyond those stars,

Plastered up above.

SIGNS

Give me a sign,

Not a blink of an eye,

True purpose doesn't hide.

Nor easily is it found,

Your reactions give traction,

Or forcefully a stop.

Give me a sign,

In the form of blessings,

I've received millions.

Finding the sign,

I am the light.

SAVOR

Soon it will pass-

Everything will be fine,

Strength and honesty,

Endure it, you will see.

Just a moment,

In your eternal life,

Savor the lessons;

Because dear, you are heaven sent.

ALLY

As darkness sets in-

Silence is my only ally;

A virtue with this horrid pain,

Never shall I cry out in agony!

I'll do just fine here,

On my own-

Withdraw your hand!

You're all living in vain surroundings;

Tainted by unworthy ignorance,

Yet they say it is bliss.

Life, for the longest of its haul;

Isn't steady, collected, nor calm.

So neither will I be!

If I am still lingering.

FLEETING

Don't dwell on what's past;

Fleeting moments-

Wither like grass.

Free your expectations;

You're free-

Save for self-limitations.

ON MY OWN

I did it on my own,

Without you-

Seeing bigger pictures.

Try and hold me back,

You're nothing but the past,

And I'm breaking through the ashes.

READY NOW

We've dreamed each-others dreams-

Are you ready?

Let's make this a reality,

Changing the course of fate.

THE COURAGE

Let go of humanly values-

Open-up to spiritual virtues,

Divine are those who understand,

Even faith can change a man.

Strength comes from self,

And trusting the unseen.

You will believe, changes are within;

Consciously courageous,

Scream out in confidence,

You are proud, destined, and free!

FINDING

Searching the skies,

Traveling the world.

But when will I find;

A place-

That I can call home?

www.ingramcontent.com/pod-product-compliance
Lightning Source LLC
Chambersburg PA
CBHW052344220526
45465CB00003BA/946